ETCETERA

BRIAN WAKE

ETCETERA
new and selected poems

HEADLAND

First published in 2011
by
HEADLAND PUBLICATIONS
38 York Avenue
West Kirby, Wirral
CH48 3JF

British Library Cataloguing in Publication Data.
A full CIP record for this book is available from the British Library
ISBN
978 1 902096 68 1

HEADLAND acknowledges the financial
assistance of Arts Council England

Printed in Great Britain by
Oriel Studios, Orrell Mount
Hawthorne Road, Merseyside L20 6NS

*The smaller mind will often lack the courage
to be dull, the bottle to be less than obvious.*

ACKNOWLEDGEMENTS

The poem 'Etcetera' first apeared in *The Poet's Perspective; Poems for Paintings in the Walker Art Gallery*, edited by Gladys Mary Coles (Headland, 2010).

Grateful acknowledgement is made to Tim Head and the Walker Art Gallery for permission to reproduce an image of *'Cow Mutations'* by Tim Head, winner of the John Moores Contemporary Painting Prize, 1987.

Thanks also to the Bridgeman Art Library for the following images and the licence to reproduce them in *Etcetera*:
In a Café, or The Absinthe, c.1875-76 (oil on canvas) by Degas, Edgar (1834-1917) Musée d'Orsay, Paris, France/ Giraudon/ The Bridgeman Art Library
The Card Players, 1893-96 (oil on canvas) by Cézanne, Paul (1839-1906) Musée d'Orsay, Paris, France/The Bridgeman Art Library.

The publisher wishes to thank Janet Wake for her photography and the design of the front cover of this book.

CONTENTS

new poems
(2009-2010)

Drink

(Degas: In a Café, or The Absinthe c. 1834-1917)

I used to glory in the spontaneity of moments
when the calculated relevance of every word
was second only to perhaps. I'd balance
the impermanency of man against the durability
of monuments. Bathe in natural delights.
I dressed for prettiness. Tied ribbons on my shoes
and envied cats their insolence, their ceaseless
searching for a square of sunlight in a quiet room.

He said he sought to win new footholds in the void
for both of us. That, in an instant, several million
images are branded on the human brain and, with them,
the conviction that all humankind is made for nothing
else except to mate, relate and feed. And not forgetting
drink, of course, I said. and he agreed. We laughed.
We drink, he said, to guard against the urge to be alone.

Ennui

(Sickert: Ennui, The Tate Gallery, London)

The smaller mind, you said, will often lack the courage
to be dull, the bottle to be less than obvious.
Each evening, after dinner, either we would sit,
both stabbing sparks like stars out of the burning wood,
with little use for ethical consistency, no time for recklessness,
or else I'd stand and listen to the wireless while he smoked
his cigar. I'd watch the painting of my father looking at us
from its frame. Every day the same.

Meticulous, I need to keep, you said, like matchsticks,
just in case, ideas in a cardboard box, notions on a bulldog-clip
and desperate measures in the sideboard drawer.

My father watches from the wall. His house built endways
to the road, he dug for victory. He planted rows and rows
of anything at all. His garden was a carnival of green.
And after dark I like to write, he used to say, if only
to rekindle into animation every circumstance connected
with myself. I celebrate exaggeration and the glass half full.

The walls in here, you said, could use a lick of paint.
Dust, you said, is gathering on the shelf.

Paradise

During the war, their breakfast, every morning
on the devastated farm, was either, nine times
out of ten, an extraordinarily renewed determination
or remorse. The cattle gone, the sheep, the horse.

Occupied the barn, searched haystacks
for the enemy and eggs. Slaughtered the hens.
Served taboos, like dogs and cats, for lunch
with yellow cabbages and rotting fish
to eat in silence but for hard bread tapping
on the dish; for gunshots in the mountains.

Unwinding bandages to bind their limbs,
they spoke of fundamental contradictions, grilling
lunch on bomb heat, ideologies and lambs
on open fire. In normal circumstances, they,
the men and women, would have headed off
to work in offices, on building sites, have driven
wagonloads of groceries to superstores or children
home from school, avoiding all entanglements,
or taught, mailed messages, sent birthday cards
or decorated living rooms, attended funerals,
put coats of paint on bedroom walls and doors.

War, and they watch the hills, not for returning
sheep or harvests, but for armoured cars,
the helicopter, shooting stars, for tall men
bearing guns and bitterness who have squatted
with begging bowls in the shadows of volcanoes;
the element of surprise, for men with prayers
and flowers in their hands and in their eyes
the gift of paradise.

Etcetera
(Tim Head: Cow Mutations, 1987)

We graze for hours through the densely structured arguments
about what is and what is not, the genesis of patterns framed
and hung for all to see. But we are prisoners.

Have taken for granted that a fundamental mark
of our distinction is the time somebody takes to understand
that we are not the cut-out clouds they thought, constrained
by all their own subjective contours, not mere inkblots
or the accidental shape of cattle, chiaroscuro cows abstracted
into analogues of what a glance reveals, but prisoners.

Some days we are reduced to inference, can only dream
the great stampede, of thundering through the landscapes
room by room, can only hope that there will be someone
to see us more than mere etceteras.

And in the evening, when everyone has gone,
when the walls we hang upon are being washed and hoofprints
scrubbed out of the polished floors, a portrait of a woman comes
with fists of grass. Now eat, she says. We do. Now, carrying a glass
of painted raindrops, drink. We drink.

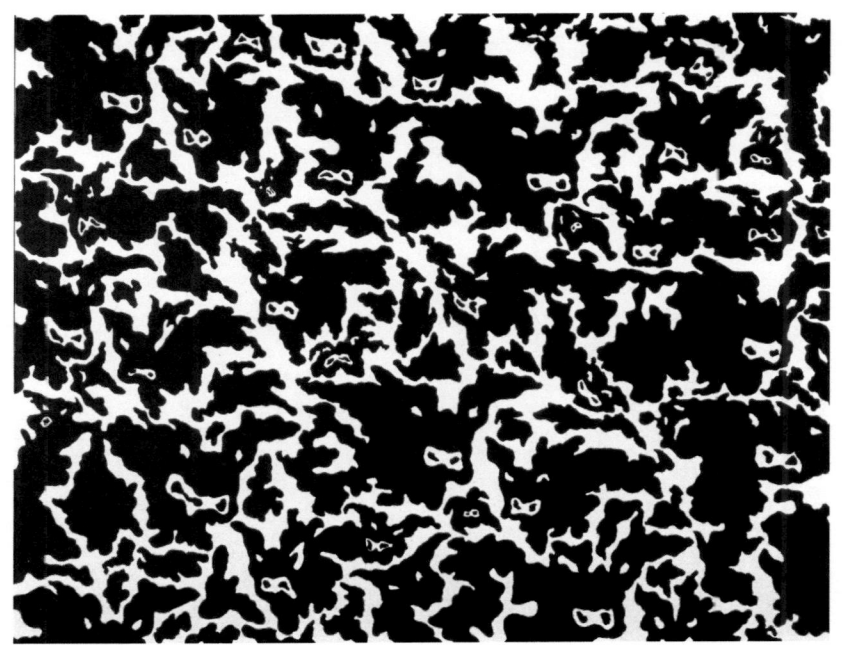

Let There Be Paul Robeson

And on the morning of the eighth day,
God, pondering the differences between
the quietness of snakes and laughter,
said, in addition to the light and darkness,
let, as well as oceans heaving with the massive
swell of fish, there be, as well as scintillating
skies, innumerable stars and beasts,
Paul Robeson.

Let us contruct him from the essences
combined of apes and mud. And let his name
be mud. And let his voice be beautiful
and let his heart be utterly immaculate.

And then an angel asked, with all of this,
would he accept advice. Yes, gladly, God
replied. Good's infinite, eternal like the sounds
we make, the voice that sings eternally.

Whose voice and heart, God said, reclining
on his eighth and very special day, could be
so beautiful who hadn't sought to know
what perfect is or asked me how to sing?

The Present Moment Lasts Three Seconds
(Miroslav Holub)

I spent my first few years climbing trees
or wanting to. And every day the same.
I knew quite clearly what I had to do.
Wore brown and green and, in my pockets,
carried aniseed or liquorice as medicine to ease
the pain when falling seemed the only way to go.

I found, from high up there, a new perspective;
the branch triangulating every seven stars,
the planetary structures and their pitted surfaces
like hearts attacked by love or by disease.

I spent my first few years climbing trees
and wanting to attain the airless heights
that birds avoid, investigate how night's black air
accumulates, breath storms where microscopic
travellers migrate from leaf to bough, their present
moment three short seconds long, eternity a day or so.

The Card Players

(Cézanne: The Card Players 1893-1996)

I fear, sitting here, despite the decent hand,
the good supply of drinks, my pipe just lit
and gypsy music in the lounge, being blindly drawn
or led by an irresistible impatience just to see
or stack or to even shuffle my good cards
into the pack and leave.

Imagination is, for me, the free pursuit of all
the latent possibilities, and yet I strive to move
towards a clearer choice between the obvious
and limitless unknown.

I often think that I have been alone too long
in knowing that the happiest of us are those
who understand, despite a certain winning hand,
how best to lose. To contemplate the chances
taken in high spirits after wine, the clowning
and the parodies, and to balance these against
the probability of ruin.

Goethe's Clock

Goethe's clock is ticking in an empty room.
He sits quite motionless. All art, then peels
a curling strip of wallpaper from a dilapidated
wall, begins, he says, from what we know
and seeks connections everywhere. All poetry
gives probability to our disjointed world.

Goethe winds his clock each afternoon
at twenty five to four. I wind the present on,
he says, the shipwrecked man ashore. I will assert
my part in what, until a moment such as this,
has been concealed. I wind a dawn of flickering
light bulbs into something more meticulous.

Goethe winds his clock against the floodgate
swelling with the pressing weight of all he knows
but fears will forget, the force of instinct, reason
and the privilege of art, the walls of books.

I wind, he says, the unexpected footsteps
in the newly fallen snow. I wind the barricades
set up against the odds of never growing old.
I wind the passive consciousness of such
impossibilities. I wind, he says, and pours
a quantity of wine into an empty glass,
the sum of almost everything I ever knew
into a time that cannot pass.

from
Into Hiding
(1993)

Adrift

My father talks of being twenty
days in an open boat. Adrift.
My father and others. War time
and the ocean was a bloodslick
clinging to continents.

They had been hit and only the dead
escaped the long days measured
by the turning boat beneath a cruel sun.
Each day a hundred hours of cracked
tongues along the chalk of teeth.

He remembers giving up, that his final
thoughts were all about a crooked,
and comfortable back yard wall
and thin but glorious lines of silver
smoke from little chimneys. In winter,
rivers of gusting snow down white
and moaning lanes. In summer, flowers
and things they wished they had done
or said.

He recalls believing themselves to be dead
yet each alive to mourn his own death.

My father talks of the years having flown,
of being twenty days adrift. His garden
is a blizzard of white roses.

Aunt

Forty years ago she was taken,
the whiff of vague Juanita, Esterlina,
fingers brown with Woodbines, away

Forty years ago, taxi, wireless, handbag,
a beret hoopla'd on. A sight to set
the curtains trembling, the street awash
with talk for weeks.

Off our hands, she marched the corridors
of her new, reluctant home, throwing
space behind with her good arm –
the bad a lance to poke at all
of which she disapproved,

And always, during visits,
through the random shape of smoke
escaping past her port pink lips,
'I'm coming home.' she'd splutter,
'home,' she'd say, 'and tell
your mother that.'

The sort that lives forever.
And now in a death cold room,
we stand, my mother and I; me
fixed upon the bloodless scowl,
the fingers Woodbine brown;
she wanting just to tuck her in,
to straighten her dead sister out.

Buried Treasure

Died at sea. The pylorus blocked-stop-suddenly-stop-kingsline-stop
was a latin we had never learned, was the ship that ran aground,
the killer, caught too late, that swam in him. The shark's unblinking
eye, the terrifying fin both shocking in the foaming depths.

Buried in Capetown. And all the kingsline stops pulled out, the snaps
in black and white, the grave, indifferent representatives on duty
in their kingsline funeral suits, compulsory. Grey wreaths,
a mourning shipmate and a black man with a spade. Disconsolate.

As kids, in 1958, we hardly felt the space my sea-going grandfather's
death had made. But rather fancied how they'd taken him ashore,
how, with their bare and bleeding hands, they'd pulled the pirate's blood
-stained cutlass from his bleeding heart, how sixteen heaving oars
had pushed the sea behind, how a beaching keel had gashed and scarred
the salt white sands of Africa and how our mother's father's corpse
was buried treasure miles and miles away.

Country Dancing

There is nothing to be frightened of, she said,
but come along and lie here on the bed.
we spoke of country dancing and of how
so very sad it was to have to dance alone,
to move in time with no-one's steps and music but your own.

But there is nothing to be frightened of, she said,
and come, my dear, and lie down on the bed.

And country dancing was the only time I ever moved.
A solitary shuffler, shadow-partnered, I improved,
danced the days away from wall to wall
and, although I often stumbled, they had taught me how to fall.

But when the dancing ended I could always hear
a voice that told me there was nothing there at all to fear.
There is absolutely nothing to be frightened of my dear.

Grinding Lanes

No mines but always coal;
the smell of coal and the smack
in the mouth of gas across
black hills. And, further on,
squat dockside cranes, their lines
spun out into the grey Mersey.

Bootle this, back street upon
back street upon back street
and gaps like missing teeth.
Back streets upon back streets
and gaps like missing teeth
A hard case place, still proud
of bomb scars, fires in blitztime.

And here, from a window high
above the sudden squares of grass,
the speckle of fog lights poking
through the shape of roads, I am
drawn to absences, to spaces
in the air where buildings pressed
and wild steam blew from a steady
flow of slithering trains. Where songs
from pubs and parlours rose
and popped like fireworks and slow,
deliberate men tugged horses,
ringing hooves and boots,
like church bells, over grinding lanes.

Horizons

Home from sea and this time home for good,
paid off and spent, my father walks around
and looks for things to do; for wood to cut or stain,
a clock to wind, a cup to swill the tea leaves from.

Seventy four and moored forever in the calm
of home, he stows adventure into sweeping floors,
sets shirts to dry full sail along the washing line,
sees silver fins that flickers in the drain,
and land ahead through days and days of rain.

Around the house, he looks for things to do,
for doors to lock, or potted plants to water or to trim,
a wall to paint horizons on.

Into Hiding

Hiding from me at bedtime, my daughter
sneezes and giggles from inside the wardrobe.
I wonder where she is, I act. Pretending
not to see her four small fingers clutching
the door. but, fearing the dark far more
than she does me, she surrenders. I gasp
in mock surprise. Soon she will be sleeping.

In Germany once
whole families hid in cupboards
while friends pretended not to see.
But, seventy years on, most would say
forget, forgive, let ancient horrors be.

Me? I am reminded tonight of the mother
who, on hearing footsteps on the stairs,
hurried her children into hiding; four hearts
thumping in a wardrobe.

Like mine, perhaps her daughter
would have giggled had she sneezed.
Sneezed and giggled, giggled and sneezed,
sneezed away four lives.

I smothered her so the others might survive.
It was Thursday, the ninth, in nineteen thirty
Nine. November, she says, I remember, thinking
even then how all her little movements
were as earthquakes when matched against
the stillnesses to come.

Kept Simple

Eighty seven, she was, or eight
years old, quite deaf and yet
we'd bawl our names as though
to rouse her from the slow
decline and stir her almost sleeping
heart, identify our kids and muddle
all her sense of time.

Like curling snapshots kept
to weave the thread of generations,
we kept her. We, my family,
she, a simple woman – mind-jammed
in between the turn of centuries.

As kids ourselves, we'd heard
how she was pulled alive
from bomb-swept streets, in nineteen
forty two, and through
the heart-storm of her mother's
sudden death.

At forty five, an orphan taken in
and kept until today when, cutting
threads at eighty odd, she prised
two centuries apart.

Open Fire

I wonder did her finger pick at dust,
her bruised eye open on to the rough stone floor
as she lay there, they said. Whether flickering
thoughts had quickened towards conclusions.

And there we were, their sons, three brothers
hearing this, before an open fire, gas hissing
from the hot coal, each seeing play streets crackling
with sparks, fire-spitting dockyards burning in the grate.

We watched them excavate vague recollections,
tear down the monuments of debris, the tapestry
of matted weeds entangling forty one or two
or was it nineteen forty four?

I wonder did her finger pick at dust, they said,
the closing eyes see light beneath the door.

Sixty Winters

After the snow,
after long quiet days of snow
and the shock of cold glass
uncurtained suddenly to silent,
still and altogether softer streets.

After all this, the yellow grass
and the last rooftop-sliding snowpile
thudding on to green-again lawns,
and cars again sluicing the grooves,
dark snowdregs spraying the pavements,
footprints spreading into dark pools.

This is my sixtieth snowtime,
sixty winters of storms and stillnesses,
and the times (between the falling
and the thaw) growing briefer,
and snowspots left unspoilt –
more difficult to find.

Small Square

And here, he said, right here,
standing in a small square
against a new brick wall,
his hands reshaping rooms.

Here, he said, eyes rising
step by step, head tilted
at invisible stairs. is where,
I think, they lay, caught
in the sudden downpour
of an iron storm and stone
but calm beneath the burning
sky, the hum of aircraft.
And here, he said, right here,
his fingers tracing brickshapes.

From imagined edges of his special
space, we watch, to rouse the sleepers
there, my cousin pushing
back through more than sixty years.

As casually as home for tea,
his heart rebuilds his mother's home
and, through the thought of debris,
goes to her and here and there
from room to room.

Snapshot

Correctly centred, boxed in, all set,
we stand, my brother and I, in a garden.
He, upright, braving the light, his neat
hair parted and wet. Me, my hand saluting
for shade, one sock down, a sight.

Of what are we dreaming as we stand
just a summer or two past the shudders
of war? He, perhaps, about what games
to play inside the broken homes,
the bomb-gouged streets, the disorder
of debris. Me, his tag-along, of simply
being there and picking up the fun
he never had.

Parts of us both have faded
into a landscape long since altered.
The grey of us into the grey of stone.
Out of this soiled snapshot we have grown,
my brother and I, from brothers into men.

Stones

Stones are surfaces, nothing else.
They cannot break except in to a thousand stones.
Smooth as air that oozes from the space we take.
Sharp as the splintered bone, a flicker of lightning.
Our touch is their structure.
They exist only on the tips of fingers.
They exist only on the tips of tongues.

Stones are the shape of water.

As warm as overwhelming tenderness or cold
as moon steel speckled against dark falling snow.

Stones are the decisions the eye makes.

Their taste is salt on the raw uncovered lip
The flavour of earth.Their dryness is a meal of cloth.
They are solid fog infrangible. They are its silence,
stones, and everywhere. Touch them and they move.
Touch them and they are moved. They survive
by being less than living things.

Your Last Spring

Awkwardly down on the lawn, and stiff
with pain, you ruffled the soil to poke the limp
shoots in and set them off with drizzle from a can.

I watched. Hot drinks were brought outside.
We drank and tea steam puffed along
with what you had to say. The sun stayed late
that day. Held on as though to give you extra
time and light to get enough things done.

By summer your garden had failed. A doom-grey
stain unlinked the chain of luscious lawns.
Nothing you had planted grew that spring
in nineteen eighty nine, while surgeons, specialists
and teams of nurses fought to scrape the flourishing
tumours from your spine.

Taking Steps

Next summer we'll sit eating bread
and cheese from a bag on the warms steps
around the Piazza della Signoria.

We'll recall today and this brown garden,
lifeless, bound inside a year of tangled grass.
Recall directions we had planned like generals
scratching strategies in the desert sand.

And we'll remember sketching, from the steps
in Florence, dreams on this hard soil in this dead
garden here.

Our eating done, we'll take whatever steps
will lead us to the highest places. Seeing, as we climb,
a tapestry of tended gardens – gardenias high
as churches, grass brushed smooth by steady winds.

No tangled webs shall weave around us then,
but only the brightest lights shall spread their silver

even into the very underneath of everything.

from
Unbuilding The Ark
(1999)

Adam & Eve Leave For The Airport

How late we set off after waiting so long to go,
he says. The bus for the airport leaves at nine.
But wait again, says she, we must water
the house-plants one last time, leave food
for the birds as the storm-clouds climb
up and over the darkening skies. One
misdemeanour, she sighs, one single slip.

Vapid winds build leaves to sudden hills.
A siren, somewhere, wails through all the bare
hedges. There is ice on the river.

How long we linger after so much time.
The bus for the airport leaves at nine.
Let me take your hand, he says, let me
dry your desperate eyes. Let us lock
this garden gate and say to hell with paradise.

Adam & Eve Take The Last Bus Home

Since Eden, said Eve, we are mortally
entwined in a web of duties. Two please,
she said, to the bus-stop nearest Paradise.
Our bags are on the rack and stuffed,
would you believe, with socks and shirts
and social obligation.

But can, my flower, you, said Adam,
say, counting his change (of circumstance
perhaps) to pay their fare, that knowledge
desires to be known and that the task of each
of us alive, together or alone, is to acquire it?
Perhaps, she said, perhaps.

Then what of love, said he, what
when the nervous, nice-to-meet-you handshake
turns the tide, and letters in a name spin
anagrams. What then? And is there ever time
to kiss?

Progress we have, perfectibility, she said,
you know all this, inbuilt, the makings
of our own downfall. Our bias, dear, is toward
sensational worsts. But let's dismiss this fact,
said Eve awakening, let us turn inevitability
and destiny on their heads, or else get off
just one stop sooner than we ever planned
and walk.

All Go

Love, imagines Eve, ironing the sleeve
of Adam's shirt, and dancing lightly
to the hissing snakes of steam, can, it would
seem, be subdued only by the intuitive,
food, she thinks, for thought, creation of art.
And pressing the collar, its essence, thinks,
is the horror of loneliness, the fear of being
alone.

From her window, Eve sees Adam
burning leaves and, in the glass, burns too.
I wonder, she imagines, if I thought of rain
would storms begin? If I thought him up
a tree would he, old grumpy boots, for godsake
get me down, be there? If I thought us back
but just a week or so ago, would leaves
be on each tree again and green and apples
and holding hands, the garden swathed with foliage,
birds sweeping through, fish in the pond.

I'll take another garment from the pile
and set it out, she thinks. He lights a cigarette.
I brand, imagining, and smoke and steam combining,
every shirt of his with love, and iron out
our differences, each frown, and leave,
in every careful fold, a poem.

Books

A good, Cain sighs, book,
counting the steps, four, five,
then resting, six, for a moment
on the seventh in his cell, is quite,
good morning sir, the purest
essence of the human soul.

I'm best inside, he says,
best locked away. I read for days
on end, the dark of Dostoyevsky
with a torch, unravelling the twists
of Joyce, unbraiding Kafka knot
by knot, strike Balzac like a match
against the wall.

Cain stacks his books, like stairs,
and climbs them to the grille. Eight,
nine, he breathes, and rests again at ten.
I get, from here, a whiff of what goes on
outside, the utmost sense of now.
he says, and then.

Catching Breath

Unable to sleep, Noah would,
on summer nights, take a glass
or two of something cool outside
and lean against his gate, watch
all the parts of dark accumulate,
the wind get set to blow, the rain
to fall, and wait.

Why don't you, Noah, someone
said, try counting sheep.
We docked, soon after dawn,
at Ararat, and every pair
of this and that came down
that gangplank like a shot,
and not so much as a by your leave,
but splitter-splatting, hoofing,
flapping, slob and bog
of steaming land.

I keep, for old time's sake,
he said, a raindrop in my hand.
I gasp at rainbows.

Clutching At Straw

An unexamined life, thought Daniel,
settling for the night on an eiderdown
of lions, is not a life at all.

I was hardly born until a little while ago,
testing the hunger of these beasts,
daring my ten-to-the dozen heart
to beat as never before.

Not anymore, he thought. Not anymore.
No more poor Daniel what's-his-name
with television seven nights a week,
adventure – someone knocking
at the door. Not anymore. Not anymore.

Up like a lark, he thought. Up like a lark.
I'll pace the cage and gauge my space,
and I'll not clutch at strands of straw
but roar, like them, for meat and even bite
the hand of anyone that feeds me.

Eve Does Breakfast Television

Well gardening really, said Eve.
I'd pick, sow, trim the edges, mow.
But always we were so tired,
so extremely tired.

We kept a horse, a cat, a dog,
some pigs and there were hens.
Adam's hat was more a bag
for eggs than ever on his head.
He took it worse than me, she said.

The lane from the farm was difficult
to drive. On Saturdays we bounced
to town. But always one or both of us
came down with something.
Sickness sought us out.

And fruit we loved. On market days
we would cram the backseat of our car
and fill the boot with fruit of every kind.
Some mornings I would find him
weeping in the garden.

Autumn is the hardest time I find.
I hear the swollen river cutting new ways
through the land. And, of course, I miss
him but people are so very kind.

Fiddling The Books

Nero knew, if anything, that Edinburgh
at festival time was his only chance of escape.
The ghostly piper on the castle wall,
the fireworks display, the buzzing throng.

Anonymity is my only hope, he said.
In bars like these I see not prison but release.
I will not have it said that I have stood,
and watched, and fiddled indeed, as lovely
Rome went up in flames.

He wondered, when he spoke, whether
anybody heard. Or, if they did, whether
anybody understood a word of what he said.
I was asleep that time in Antium, you know.
He chalked, instead of steak and kidney pie
three ninety five, and chips, on to a board
above the bar. I was an emperor you see.
I was a king with music in my soul.

At closing time, he sits outside, and sings.
Defined by sparkling stars and bonfire light.
I had, until today, known only victory,
known only win, success, hip-hip hooray, applause.
I wish, he said, I could have understood a little
more of not, a little more of no, a little less of yes.

Fifty Hats

A hunter, Daniel ponders, looking down
from his safe tree, its claw-scored bough
now barkless in the quiet heat, that can impose
on any creature all the power of the human mind,
will surely know how, in its terror, in its quest
to get away, a lion might behave.

And sometimes, Daniels thinks, it could be said,
and balancing ideas on his head like fifty hats,
that we are at our bravest when afraid, wisest
when we do not know and steadier for having
fallen down.

He contemplates, from his high tree,
the need to give and take, blend most with least
and learn to hang competitive advantages
on the wall, like coats off for a fight.
To face even a lion beast to beast.

Homeless And Hungry, Please Help

Samson's dog thinks it is very kind
of those who knew his master to remember.
Nice, he barks, of you to seek this
unfrequented place to visit him.

I must pretend, he thinks, for his sake,
that I see, that all our walks around
the millwheel are on awesome mountain
paths and he is treading dangerous ground.

Pretend, too, that the sound of grinding
is a lion's roar, the click of brazen fetters
over stone, change thrown into his hat
and that the wailing operas of slaves,
wolves hungry at the city gate.

On my day off it's his turn to take me.
We walk for miles and he might sing,
might tackle the steeper hills, might
sometimes stop me in my tracks
to scrape a message in the sand.

Texture, it might say, and form, and shaking
me from head to toe, are more important
than the words we use. The shape of what
we write can sometimes mean far more
than what we say... Alas, thinks Samson's
dog. Alas, alas, alas, my master sometimes
talks out of the jawbone of his ass.

I Never Did Think

I never did think highly
of the sea, said Noah,
but used it as a means
to come and go heroically,
pack suitcases and kiss
someone goodbye, wishing
all the best to neighbours
passing by, someone hello.

Against the silver walls
of icebergs, I, he said,
throwing bits of bread
to feed the birds, have heard
the echo of a storm more
clearly than the storm itself.

I sometimes find, said Noah,
relaxing with a paper at his gate,
my eyes fixed firmly on a shape
created not by what is there
before me, but by all the absences
of objects in between.

Jonah

Whale and me, we breasted the same weed.
Some nights I'd swim right out of his arse
and take the evening air on the shores, said Jonah,
of Tarshish. Good times.

I'd goggle hunt for pearls or shark ride
into unlooted palaces, he said, thread a route
through flurrying fish, harpooning them for lunch.
I'd poach them in his gut. We'd celebrate.

On Saturdays, he said, we'd sizzle through
the ocean top and whale and me would belly flop,
we'd brush the same uneasy reed. And people,
since, have never been enough, have seldom done.

There is more to the sea than water, than silence
and danger, more to the dark. No friends, these
days, for me, said Jonah, I look and see only
myself in a mirror of strangers.

Lazarus Meets The Press

What worries me, said Lazarus,
trapping flies in a glass,
brushing dust from his shirt,
what concerns me most of all,
wiping dirt from his eye, counting
fingers – eight, nine, ten, what
worries me now is doing it again.

I'm lumbered now, he said, saddled
with the signs, the killer clues, chest
pains, the fizzling arm, forgetfulness,
the fingernails turned porcelain,
cholesterol, the horror of incontinence
and lumps and loss of weight. The calm
before the storm, the sense of doom,
things that go bump in the night,
a world turned waiting room.

Asked why by the man from the BBC.
got it over with you see. Out like a light,
he said, goodnight and all the lights
were out, and in whatever sky
I tumbled through, not a single star
nor any blue.

Leading The Blind

Blind himself, yet Samson's dog
made absolutely no concession
to the dark, but would cross, and bark,
the river on a bridge of crocodiles.
Neither he nor they aware
that either he or they were there.

Without him I'd be lost, said Samson
to a slave, without him there would be,
no midday walks along the iron-hot
mountain paths, no waves of flower
scent bristling, sound of breathing.

But how can he, thought Samson's dog,
think that, who never moves except
to tread a deep and deeper groove,
and every day, around the millwheel?
How can he say that all we have
encountered on our walks is something
like a tragic sense of life carved out
of stone, imperfection written in the way
a desert sand is accidentally blown
by quite indifferent wind?

I dream, thought Samson's dog,
not of the ecstasy of human kind,
the simultaneous ripening and rotting
of the human minds, of creatures living
out their brief existences in harmony,
or Samson dying on his feet.
I contemplate the equal deaths
of emperors and kings and slaves
and, on our daily walks, will sniff
the ground for any whiff of graves
or bones that might be good
enough to eat.

Lost For Words

And what, thought Samson's dog,
stopping to sniff at stones and strum
his fur for irritating fleas, is conversation
now to him but noise upon the air?

I sometimes get, he thinks, a whiff
of what could be, a sudden gush
of possibilities, imagining, for him,
a speck of light to prick the dark
of his quite unimaginable despair.

I would like to flood, and snapping
at a dilatory fly, before he coughs
and stops to spit and burst the morning
blister with a stick, his mind with yes
and certainly, his heart with wonderful.

Moses Begins To Feel His Age

Moses came to understand
that any mention of his name
could instigate a plague
of questions, ridicule.

Paper shop, post office,
waiting for a bus, sometimes
on the top of the mountain,
sometimes thinking about
the old days, old friends
and the parting of the ways,
and voices would call, *Hey,
Moses, tell us about Manna,
Moses, the Red Sea, Moses.
Hey there Moses, strike a rock,
Moses, Golden Calf, Moses.
Tablets, Moses, of stone.*

And so it is, he said, that now
I live alone and quietly,
an ancient man, all memories
distorted in a doom-blue cloud
of jumbled times. I've outgrown
the old crowd. I read a bit,
the papers mainly, magazines,
odd book. I love the soaps,
love *Question Time, The News*
but most of all *Have I Got News
For You.*

Raining Cats & Dogs

What's with, thought Noah, these hands,
hesitating; these once phenomenal fingers
that could weave the Ark through seething
ocean walls?

What's with these eyes that once foresaw
the bank of brooding clouds prepare, he thought,
their universal bucketful of rain?

What's with this daft expression, slack gob,
slobber dangling from a stupid mouth?

What's with my handkerchief not being
where I thought it was, my comb not there
to comb my hair?

And am I not the very last, returning home,
great bumbling mammoth out, he thought,
of whose incredible tusks so many smaller minds
have carved their ivory towers?

What's with my hard of hearing, slow to get there,
wet my trousers way of taking far too long
to say exactly what I mean?

Before the rain, thought Noah, I was sharp,
precise and clear in every way. The excitingness
of being had not quite withdrawn itself.

And what's with me, afraid of crossing roads,
who booted rivers into touch, of slipping
on the snow who danced on icebergs?

Throwing Stones

Lucky for you, lucky for you
I lived not in the glass house
of my fathers, not in the bricks
and mortar, in the mud and bullets
of another time, David would say.
Lucky for you I did not live
in a glass house. And, licking
his lips and thumbs, would wipe
away the marks of blood
and clean his favourite stone.

Goliath, you might say, could
never have known what hit him.
Expected mighty forces, big things;
not breezes but storms, eagles
not sparrows, had watched the sky
for the thousand slings and arrows,
kept one eye out for a wall of men
and horses, snorting, that would charge
to cut him down.

I am dropping, said David, a line
to one I have not seen for years;
hides out, they say, in the mountains,
lives off the land, eats birds,
takes avalanches with a pinch of salt.

With reference to the giant, I shall say,
there is nothing left to fear, I loved
you then and love you still. He is killed
in battle and the coast is clear, come home.
Wear something warm for the journey
for the summer nights deceive.
I am living now near Shococh,
a little way past Ephes-dammin, a little
off the beaten track, just a stone's throw
from the river.

Unbuilding The Ark

Mine is the insoluble dilemma,
said Noah, unbuilding the Ark,
and launching four-by-twos,
like rafts, into the new world,
the death of the heart.
I care, he said, for nothing
without rain, and everything
is falling, now, apart.

Nail by nail, unmakes his ship.
Better, he would say, that I
should hammer these into my hands
and feet, that I should hang myself
to bits of boat wood on a hill
and pierce my side.

His visitors arrive in twos.
They talk among themselves.
And how are we, they ask,
each other, how are we today.
Mine is the insoluble dilemma,
he would whisper, the death
of the heart, he would say.

Unfit For Battle

And when I blink, doctor,
the world goes out like a light,
doctor. When I close my eyes
there is more, doctor, than
darkness, doctor, or do not
speak and there is, doctor,
universal silence.

Blow on a ram's horn,
doctor, and walls tumble.
I sense eternity, doctor,
and it's frightening, doctor,
help me.

Joshua's GP holds Joshua's
shaking hands. Take hold,
he says, take hold and let
the desert sands become
the landscape storms dictate.
And stand apart and only
watch. Even the flogged
blind horse, if only by some
chance, pulls a significant
cart. Undo your eyes,
Mister Joshua, undo your eyes
and let me see your heart.

Washed Ashore

On Sundays whale would gulp great storms
of air and spend all day spreadeagled
on the ocean bed, flat out. And I, instead
of sleeping off the frenzied razzmatazz
of Saturday, would curl inside the bubble
of his breath then rise and dart, said Jonah,
from the depths of who-knows-where,
the essence of the ocean's heart, from there
on to the orange beaches of the west;
Saint-Jean-de-luz, Royan.

On Mondays whale, again, would watch me
from the ocean floor, would surface suddenly
transformed into a gulping precinct, a deadly
route for bungled fish, for flotsam, jetsom,
submarines, for tuna dazzled by their own hypnotic
dance, for blind men who had fallen in,
for lovers who had fallen out, for falling stars
that nobody had caught

I always thought, said Jonah, that I understood
and justified, disguised as something washed ashore,
the total absence of remorse. I saw how yesterday
(and soon) could seem ridiculous. I watched
the swaying seaweed girls go walking arm in arm
along the promenade, saw sea wind spattering
the jetty stones with rain.

from
Raining Upwards
(2000)

Chekhov's Sandwiches

Chekhov's sandwiches
were often silences
placed either side of sound.
A snack prepared
instinctively
and, as spectator's found,
one he would either eat
or else would balance
on his head.

I like, he thought, to test
the weight of nothing said
against the repetition
of absurdities.

Chopin's Mirror

Chopin's mirror was another room
in which he would prefer, instead
of harsh reality, inconsequential
conversations, ravelled melodies,
instead of rocking chairs, to be.
Handkerchiefs uncurling in a grate.

I wait, he said, in there for silence
to imagine harmonies itself. I sit for hours
on a most uncomfortable chair and pack
into whatever I might think, subordinate
associations, notions far too difficult
for me to understand except as little tunes.

Knowing Van Gogh

Vincent's mother's garden was all things
to everyone; a place in which he, as a boy,
had grown impatient with the muddled pace
of change, had sat and contemplated,
testing nails for pain along the fence,
and thorns. I hold the natural conditions,
he would say, of all created things
to be the vital part of ecstasy.

All yellow summer, she would bake,
and from her cottage window, sell potatoes
to the villagers. While he would grapple
with the structural significance of logs
stacked in a pile, his brother feeding
scraps to dogs, diagonals.

By golden autumn he would be engulfed
in swamps of grey and cobalt blue,
by strange yet palpable agglomerations
of fantastic cloud which he could only stand
and watch his mother wander, lonely, through.

As for him, if he were only half the boy,
his brother was. If he could care as much
for watering the plants, she said, pathetic dogs,
as for aesthetic mysticism, soil as for remorseful
courtesies for people who have failed,
the clearing of a garden path as much as being
mesmerised by all the greens and golds
that glitter from disintegrating leaves.
His falling in and, worst of all, his falling out
of love, then Vincent would be something
to write home about.

Looking At Stones

Only ever looked at stones, saw in them
all he needed to know, all there was to recall.
Wore a uniform still, though no longer at war.
They are, he would exclaim, each one of them,
a sort of frozen sea engrained with waves,
the evidence of form, the memory of many
things that now no longer move.

He would stare and travellers would, passing,
stop and scratch their heads and some would leave
him bread or pour a drop of wine into his jar.

The essence, he would tell them, of a simple stone
can never be destroyed. No matter how perpetual
the gush of waterfalls, determined children are with
sticks, no matter how the urging grass might push,
it is re-formed somehow and re-arranged
as obstinate forever beats it with another stone.

Rembrandt

That's certainly a wolf
I, catching sight of Rembrandt
through a window, thought
he said. The buggers at the door.

And yet I have to paint
for almost 24, said Rembrandt,
hours a day. I paint, he said,
self consciousness.

I stake my life on drawing
it towards the very moment
when I might just understand
myself a little more – or care.

I paint to find, he said, a way
to help me sleep and to reduce
the deaths of those I love,
to something I can bear.

from
So What?
(2004)

A Cat's Life

His afternoons were spent full stretch
while waiters unpiled wicker chairs
and set them out in rows, scrubbed
café tables clean.

I dream of pyramids of aubergines
and lemons, carnations on the flower
stalls, swallows skimming the pool,
the smell of brioches from the bakery,
the sound of reed curtains jingling
in the hairdresser's.

I sometimes, he, full stretch, would
think, that after all a cat's life
in the country would be best.
A scrounging present pleasure
either sleeping or else killing
time among the fish heads. Nights
invariably cold and mornings noisy
with the arguments of streams.

Dancing The Mumbo Jumbo

His radio would only ever play,
it plays, he'd say, what I, what he,
that is, would like to hear. Would
play the danger of responsibility,
the music of a ragged coat, the ring
of change in pockets, dusty shoes,
the intuitions of irregularity. Good
news.

Instead of radical analysis, instead
of broadcasting, like football scores,
elaborate remoteness three, disorder nil,
or perturbation one, quiescence two
his radio announced what he already knew,
and life, it said, is far too short for art.

No tightropes over vast obscurities,
his radio would only state the obvious.
Would have him sprawled inside
the music of a favourite chair, feet up
with bars of chocolate and a glass or two
of sparkling poetry. Would have him dance
the mumbo jumbo like a fool.

Eating Her Head Off

My mother never would, when even at her absolutely
lowest ebb, consume a tiny bowl of soup. A drop
of chicken, celery or vegetable was out. I'd eat,
she'd say, for those who won't, my way, through
all the dark routes of despair, imaginary mutton
served with gravy, trays of cakes and fruit, a nest
of solid hardboiled eggs.

I'd eat into the crowd, she'd say, of natural events
and even guzzle rare occasions like a fiend. I'd eat
the probability that nothing ever happens which
has never been foreseen. I sometimes hope, she'd say,
and consequently eat the thought of growing old,
the passive consciousness of possibilities to which,
until my stomach aches, all values must belong.

I'd eat the empty house with chairs unmoved for centuries,
the ghosts inside and last, in there, song anybody sang.
I'd eat the cigarette that smoulders on, the barricades set up
against the hopeless odds. I'd eat the smiling fingernail,
the crescent moon, the grey, she said, dyed-blonde hairs
stranded in a comb.

Going Away To Sea

My father, every Saturday, would like to speculate
but keep an eye, test fantasies against the absolutely
ordinary, if against the obvious, on all the shifting
scenery of afternoon.

His father, he would say, had hornpiped home from war.
Quite terrified and prematurely grey and, some have said,
sailed home inside the upside down of what had been
a table set for lunch.

His father, he would say, sailed home inside a piano
buoyed by music he had learned to play. A good old guy
that wet his whistle on the waters of the moon. Sailed
waterfalls and isolation, snatched at flowers going by.

My father, mine would say, sailed every sea, self-consciousness,
the oceans of alone, sailed all my love in letters,
ships in dry dock, sailed possibility, sailed promises,
the permanent illusion. My father sailed the farewell kiss,
sailed must be off, sailed see you soon. A good old guy,
and wet his whistle on the waters of the moon.

Goldfish

He taps, each morning, on the glass.
I play the fish and dash my skull
against the indeterminable lines
of little choice.

I try to think that there exists
the perfect possibility of happiness.
I swim in order only to please him.
I swim to cheer him up, and also,
if the truth were known, perhaps
to wear my way out of the bowl.

After breakfast he will often sit
and contemplate the pattern of his day.
A man, he'll say, might find
(I dance the dance of tidal waves)
that he is living upside down,
outside the boundaries of love
(I dance applause) and, with his head
set firmly in a book or goldfish bowl,
see separation as a kiss of glass
between us all.

Half A Dozen Presents

Half asleep some nights, and blocks
of car light scanning every part
of darkness on the bedroom wall,
I knew that in such things as love,
or what could lead me to a knowledge
of it, lay my only hope.

Your father, I would, sleeping, hear
somebody telling me, would, if he could,
have given half a dozen presents
for a single moment of a reconstructed past.

Neither here, then, nor there, I would shine
my need for him like torch light into empty dark,
imagine where, for so much time, he ever was.
And every ship became my father
on the breathless risings and the swell
and easy fall of love.

And every ship, my father on the absences
and oceansful of possibilities, the measure
of itself determined by a shadow on a bedroom
wall. And every ship, my father hurting me
so gently that I never felt a thing. Hurting me
so gently that I felt no pain at all.

His Garden

His garden was a place
where nothing seemed,
except anxiety, to grow, and so,
he said, I plant stupidity now
and row upon row of looking out
for number one.

I plant, and nothing ever takes,
pretentiousness, efficiency regimes,
I plant the urge to be alone,
alone itself, and lines of disappointment.
I plant, he said, the calculated
relevance of every word, disharmony,
the natural conditions of created things.

I plant not only this and that,
a muddled sort of goodness
or goodbye, the timeless imminence,
the rapid pace of change, I plant
the eye on chance, the question marks
of falling rain, the pouring doubts,
but also what I cannot bear to face.

His garden was a place
where nothing seemed,
except anxiety, to grow.

Imperceptible Raskolnikov

Each afternoon, the almost imperceptible
Raskolnikov, his collar hiding every sign
of what he thought, his hat pulled down,
arrived to eat a meagre breakfast at a hot-dog
stand and drink, from someone else's cup,
whatever was left over from the night before.

To him, the world appeared nothing more
than what he saw through holes punched
through a newspaper. I do not represent,
he said, spilling drops of vodka from a cup,
the rest of you, the human spirit snatching
at its only chance, for bits, brushed up, of love.
I do not say that we should look the other way
until fate strikes but that it is the privilege
of art to overstep the mark. Exaggerate.

Each afternoon, Raskolnikov arrived to eat.
I'll wait, he said, forever if I must for anyone
to leave a half-filled cup of anything to drink.
We are, if only we could understand, not
as restrained by all the old taboos
as we would think.

It's Only Me

Always much too loud,
my mother's since-school friend, for me.
Too hale, by far, and hearty. Her voice
at the door would always guarantee to send
me packing, skedaddling for the dark
beneath the stairs.

But sometimes she would visit us and weep,
and only cups and cups and cups of tea
could keep her from despair. And I would
edge out of my darkness then to watch
her fold and fold again her handkerchief,
and frame an hour of tears inside
a hundred squares.

At other times we'd, all of us, catch trains
to trundle here and there with sandwiches
and flasks of something hot, weave pinewoods
into plaits of summer afternoons and dance
all day like dragonflies.

Today she died. And how she would have loved
to have been the one that popped her carpet slippers
on and hurried round with such a tale to tell,
such news. It's only me she might have said.

The teacup clinks a mourning-bell sound just for her.
My mother's handkerchief is folded on a chair.

Mister Cummings He Say Ha

Hey kid, he'd say, you got me down
as the rangy pelota player with the long
Etruscan face? You gotta be joking.

Hey kid, he'd say, you got me down
as what the hell? You got me blowing
who-cares smoke rings in a hotel corridor.
A solitary shadow on the hotel floor? Ha.

Each evening, double-e would stretch
his legs down Patchin Place, New York.
Hey kid, and venomously acting, squeak
the east side tough, know what I'm saying,
of his mouth, hey kid, you wanna know
what lonely is? I'll tell you fucking lonely.

Bars are lonely, kid, and tears exquisitely
unshed, and me so generously sad.
The sudden yearning for a far door opening,
he'd say, and footsteps growing fainter
on the hopeless stairs. That's fucking lonely.

Proust's Brother

We neither could, Proust's brother said,
and backing in with drinks and disinfected
handkerchiefs, repeat the past, despairingly,
nor leave it as it was but had to modify the lot
to fit the shape of what we had become.

We like, almost until it cracks, to tap
at certainty, and bounce the ball of absolutely
up and down until it bursts into a snow
of question marks, to reconstruct, if only pebbles
on a beach, to place the obvious a little out of reach
and change the course of probably.

At nine o'clock, eight fifty nine is just as gone
as highwaymen, as water on the moon,
and neither he nor I have ever known
the solid structure of a frozen heart
to be dissolved by anything but love;
or memorable lines, like his, across a thousand
pages, to lead us anywhere but, smackbang, back
to where we had begun.

So What?

I'm buggered, said my father, carrying binbags
out for Wednesday's collection, if I will stand
and watch the ripening, yet not despair, and rotting
of the human mind. Bits of nibbled chicken,
tea left, sandwiches unfinished, in a cup, the mail,
the milk, the newspapers, the utter rigmarole.

There may, he said, be more to all of this
than they let on, I wouldn't know, but whether,
and a broken plate, there is, an empty box, or not,
the hollow egg-shells, kitchen roll, so what!

Walking Stick

I cannot, he would rage, take any more these days,
without a stick, than half a dozen steps, and often
these are only where the stick itself would wish to go.

Stuck in the mud, he'd say, and jinxed, that's me,
and I, for what has seemed like centuries, and without love,
tread dreadful crannies around the points I have to make.

I write, he would explain, in order to maintain
an equilibrium between the very height of passion
and the grey slug moments, awful dog shit of despair.

I write to make the passive consciousness of possibility,
he'd say, to which all values must belong, appear complete.
I drink to make ends meet.

It has been, dare I say, a good deal less than wonderful,
my life, unfair, these morbid, mental growths I've had to bear,
unutterably sad. But kind, he said, of you to come.

The doctors here are marvellous but mad.

Others

Flaubert's Broken Roof

Flaubert's broken roof was silent cinema, the silver screen.
His public crouched between the dislocated slates and ribs
of joists stripped bare, found holes to watch him through.
And saw, from there, the film of as much a book as any
he would write.

I hold, he'd say to wild applause, the natural conditions
of created things to be the vital part of undiluted ecstasy.
I balance every word, to cheers, each sentence I create,
as he unfolded towels for an evening bath, turned back
the covers on his bed or combed his hair, against the weight
of all the happiness I never knew. Count every syllable
as proof of what I do, as evidence of all I've ever read.

I cannot praise, he'd indicate to hoots of joy, enough a fellow
who might teach me how I might best understand myself,
and picking flecks of dandruff from his comb, or strands of hair,
or praise him less for telling me what I should obviously know.

Rwanda 1994

He fills, with pink and simmering dregs,
a yellow plastic can. And Lake Muhazi
fills again with water bleeding through
the pot-shot bullet holes. He quite ignores,
offshore, the bleached and, face-down,
bloated corpse that floats like lumber,
turns like clock hands telling time.

A boy of eight or nine gun-rattling,
mortar-shattering years, dripping oceans
from a yellow plastic can, dripping trails
of pink and simmering dregs along a path
to where his parents sleep.

He takes Lake Muhazi, weeping
through the bullet holes, to sprinkle,
now with love and hopeful lake drops,
life again into their frozen eyes.

That'll Be The Day

I sit sometimes, and summer rain
makes accidental music in the yard,
knee-deep in a bewildering array of facts
and concepts which, for all I know,
could overwhelm a better man than me.
I feel the cello-straining-string
and croaking gloom of all that anyone
can hardly bear. Laugh?

I like, he thought, to throw myself
completely in to anything impossible.
The television on, my bare feet in a bowl
of fundamental insecurity, a sandwich
in my hand. Cheese. Onions. Laugh?

I sometimes don't believe, he thought,
a word of what I think and wonder
if, whatever I may question or profoundly
doubt, is ultimately all there is to know.
Me, laugh? That'll be the day.